DOGS SET II

Collies

Stuart A. Kallen

ABDO & Daughters

visit us at
www.abdopub.com

Published by Abdo & Daughters, 4940 Viking Drive, Suite 622, Edina, Minnesota 55435.

Copyright © 1998 by Abdo Consulting Group, Inc., Pentagon Tower, P.O. Box 36036, Minneapolis, Minnesota 55435 USA. International copyrights reserved in all countries. No part of this book may be reproduced in any form without written permission from the publisher.

Printed in the United States.

Cover Photo credits: Peter Arnold, Inc.
Interior Photo credits: Peter Arnold, Inc.

Edited by Bob Italia

Library of Congress Cataloging-in-Publication Data

Kallen, Stuart A., 1955-
        p. cm. -- (Dogs. Set II.)
        Includes index.
        Summary: Describes the physical characteristics and habits of
        these gentle herding dogs and the care they require as a pet.
        ISBN 1-56239-573-4
        1. Collie--Juvenile literature.   [1. Collie.   2. Dogs.]
        I. Title.   II. Series: Kallen, Stuart A., 1955-   Dogs. Set II.
        SF429.C6K25   1998
        636.737'4--dc21   97-15654
                                                                CIP
                                                                AC

Contents

Dogs and Wolves— Close Cousins

Dogs have been living with humans for more than 12,000 years. Today, millions of dogs live in the world. Over 400 **breeds** exist. And, believe it or not, all dogs are related to wolves. Some dogs—like tiny poodles or Great Danes—may look nothing like the wolf. But under their skin, every dog shares many feelings and **traits** with wolves.

The dog family is called Canidae, from the Latin word *canis*, meaning "dog." The canid family has 37 **species**. They include foxes, jackals, wild dogs, and wolves.

Opposite page: All dogs are related to the wolf.

Collies

Collies come from the area of northern England and Scotland. Dogs like collies were probably brought to that area by Roman invaders around 500 B.C. During the 1800s, people bred dogs to help them move their sheep and cows through different pastures. Farmers selected dogs that were gentle, strong, and smart. The collies were used for herding and guarding farm animals.

The collie got its name from the sheep it worked around. "Col" is an old Anglo-Saxon word that means "black". Scotland's black-faced sheep were called "colleys." The dog that herded and drove them was called a "colley dog." As the years passed, the spelling was changed to collie.

The first purebred collie was bred in England in the early 1800s. England's Queen Victoria loved the collie

and made the **breed** very popular in mid-nineteenth century. Collies also were very popular in America. The Collie Club of America was started in 1886. It later became the American Kennel Club.

In 1945, Eric Knight's novel *Lassie Come Home* was made into a movie. Lassie, a collie, was the name of the dog. Several Lassie movies were made. In the 1960s, "Lassie" was a popular American television show.

A border collie used for herding sheep.

What They're Like

Collies are sweet, gentle, and faithful. They are one of the smartest **breeds** of dogs. They love people and make great pets for children. Collies were used to herd animals for many centuries. They still do, with very little training.

Collies are not timid dogs. If they sense danger they will spring to action. Collies are brave but will not attack without good reason. Every year collies are given awards for heroic deeds. Collies have been awarded for saving more than 50 people at different times. They have fought off wild animals, prevented drownings, and alerted people to fires and burglaries.

Opposite page: Collies are brave dogs and have saved many people.

Coat and Color

The collie has a straight, coarse outercoat. The undercoat is soft and furry. The hair on the tail is long and bushy.

There are four colors for collies: Sable and White, Tri-color, Blue Merle, and White. A Sable and White collie is light golden and white. A Tri-color is mostly black with some Sable and White. A Blue Merle is marbled with blue-gray and black, mixed with Sable and White. A White collie is mostly white with some sable, tri-color, or blue-merle markings.

The eyes of the collie are almond-shaped, medium-sized, and dark in color. Blue merles may have two different colored eyes. They may be blue, brown, or gray.

A collie's outer coat is straight and coarse.

Size

Collies are medium-sized dogs. Males may weigh from 60 to 75 pounds (27 to 34 kg). Females may weigh from 50 to 65 pounds (23 to 30 kg).

Male collies are from 24 to 26 inches (61 to 66 cm) at the shoulder. Female collies are from 22 to 24 inches (56 to 61 cm).

Collies have medium-sized heads. The neck is firm, muscular, and long. The ears are folded except when the dog is alert. Then they point upwards.

The body of the collie is firm, with a deep chest, and long, straight legs. The paws are small, but the pads are tough. The tail has an upward twist and is carried low when the dog is resting. When the dog is excited, it carries its tail high, but not over its back.

Collies point their ears
upward when they are alert.

Care

Collies make happy members of any family. They are lovable, loyal, and proud.

Like any dog, a collie needs the same things a human needs: a warm bed, food, water, exercise, and lots of love.

Collies have long hair that needs to be brushed often. Their bushy tails may become tangled with burrs. Because of their hair, collies need to be bathed often.

All dogs need shots every year. These shots stop diseases such as **distemper** and **hepatitis.**

As a member of your household, your dog expects love and attention. Collies enjoy human contact. They love to be taken for walks where they can run and explore.

Collies make happy members of any family. The dogs in this photo are bearded collies.

Feeding

Like all dogs, collies like to eat meat. But collies need a well-balanced diet. Most dog foods—dry or canned—will give the dog proper **nutrition.**

When you buy a puppy find out what it has been eating and continue that diet. A small puppy needs four or five small meals a day. By six months, it will need only two meals a day. By one year, a single evening feeding will be enough.

Collies must be exercised every day so they do not gain weight. Walking, running, and playing together will keep you and your dog happy and healthy. Give your dog a hard rubber ball to play with.

Like any animal, collies need fresh water. Keep water next to the dog's food bowl and change it daily.

All dogs need a well-balanced diet to stay healthy.

Things They Need

A dog needs a quiet place to sleep. A soft dog bed in a quiet corner is the best place for a collie to sleep. Collies should live indoors. If the dog must live outside, give it a dry, **insulated** dog house.

Collies love to play and explore. A fenced-in yard is the perfect home for the dog. If that is not possible, use a chain on a runner.

In most cities and towns, a dog must be leashed when going for a walk. It will also need a license. A dog license has the owner's name, address, and telephone number on it. If the dog runs away, the owner can be called.

Opposite page: Collies love to play and explore.

Puppies

A collie can have up to eight puppies. The dog is **pregnant** for about nine weeks. When she is ready to give birth, she prefers a dark place away from noises. If your dog is pregnant, give her a strong box lined with an old blanket. She will have her puppies there.

Puppies are tiny and helpless when born. They arrive about a half hour apart. The mother licks them to get rid of the birth sacs and to help them start breathing. Their eyes are shut, making them blind for their first nine days. They are also deaf for about ten days.

Dogs are **mammals**. This means they drink milk from their mother. After about four weeks, puppies begin to grow teeth. Separate them from their mother and give the puppies soft dog food.

A collie can have up to eight puppies.

Glossary

breed: a grouping of animals with the same traits.

coat: the dog's outer covering of hair.

distemper: a contagious disease of dogs and certain other animals caused by a virus.

hepatitis (hep-uh-TIE-tis): an inflammation of the liver caused by virus.

insulation (in-suh-LAY-shun): something that stops heat loss.

mammal: a group of animals, including humans, that have hair and feed their young milk.

nutrition (new-TRISH-un): food; nourishment.

pregnant: with one or more babies growing inside the body.

species (SPEE-sees): a kind or type.

trait: a feature of an animal.

veterinarian: a doctor trained to take care of animals.

Internet Sites

The Border Collie Homepage
http://mendel.berkeley.edu/dogs/bcs.html
This site is a must read for anyone thinking of getting a Border Collie. BCs are wonderful dogs, but require a lot of time, attention and exercise. If you are not completely familiar with the Border Collie, you must read this information!

Collies: Back to the Future
http://izebug.syr.edu/~gsbisco/collie.htm
The purpose of this website is to provide sources of information about the history of the collie breeds (breeds that were developed from the old working collie of the British isles) in order to encourage preservation of important functional, physical, mental, behavioral and aesthetic characteristics for the future.

Valiant Collie Homepage
http://www.ptialaska.net/
~valiantindexhtml#anchor1311674
Collie Breeder. Collie Information. Collie Pictures. Collie Stories. Collie Fiction. Collie Sales. Collie Health Concerns. Before You Buy a Collie. Rescue Collies. For all Collie Information! VALIANT COLLIES.

These sites are subject to change. Go to your favorite search engine and type in Collie for more sites.

Index